The True Story of

THE BATTLE OF LEXINGTON AND CONCORD

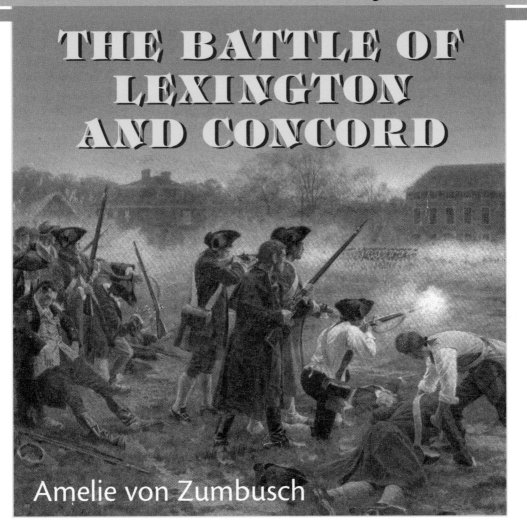

Amelie von Zumbusch

PowerKiDS
press.

New York

For my father, who always remembers the rude bridge

Published in 2009 by The Rosen Publishing Group, Inc.
29 East 21st Street, New York, NY 10010

First Edition

Editor: Nicole Pristash
Book Design: Kate Laczynski
Photo Researcher: Nicole Pristash

Photo Credits: Cover, pp. 1, 15 © Getty Images, Inc.; pp. 5, 9, 13, 17, 21 © Superstock.com; pp. 7, 11, 19 © North Wind/North Wind Picture Archives.

Library of Congress Cataloging-in-Publication Data

Zumbusch, Amelie von.
    The true story of the Battle of Lexington and Concord / Amelie von Zumbusch. — 1st ed.
        p. cm. — (What really happened?)
    Includes bibliographical references and index.
    ISBN 978-1-4042-4480-1 (library binding)
    1. Lexington, Battle of, Lexington, Mass., 1775—Juvenile literature. 2. Concord, Battle of, Concord, Mass., 1775—Juvenile literature. I. Title.
    E241.L6Z86 2009
    973.3'311—dc22

                                    2008003491

Manufactured in the United States of America

CONTENTS

What Was the Battle of Lexington and Concord?......4

The Colonies and Taxes...6

Protests 8

Warnings from Boston 10

The Minutemen 12

Who Shot First? 14

On to Concord...16

The Long March Back 18

Freedom..20

What Really Happened? 22

Glossary 23

Index 24

Web Sites..24

WHAT WAS THE BATTLE OF LEXINGTON AND CONCORD?

On April 19, 1775, men from Lexington, Massachusetts, lined up on Lexington's **common**. They had been warned, or told, that British **soldiers** were coming from Boston. The villagers thought the British might fight them. However, they did not know that the fighting there and in nearby Concord would become the first battle of the American Revolution.

The battle's story has been told often, but time has twisted some facts. Many people are **confused** about how many colonists fought, how they knew the British were coming, and who fired the first shot. Let's take a look at this important battle and find out the truth!

The battle of Lexington and Concord was the first battle of a war that would end with the colonies becoming the United States.

THE COLONIES AND TAXES

In 1775, the towns of Lexington and Concord were part of a British colony, called the Province of Massachusetts. A colony is a place that is ruled by another country. Massachusetts was one of several colonies in North America that were claimed by the British.

From 1754 to 1763, Great Britain and France fought a war, called the French and Indian War, over their North American colonies. This war left Great Britain in need of money. The British **Parliament** created, or made, taxes to raise money in the colonies. The colonists had no say in this, and the taxes made them angry.

In 1765, Britain created the Stamp Act. The act put a tax stamp on paper goods, such as newspapers and playing cards. Some colonists set fire to the stamps in anger.

PROTESTS

Throughout the colonies, Americans **protested** the new British taxes. Colonists also refused to buy goods shipped from Britain, since they were taxed. In December 1773, Bostonians dressed as Native Americans threw taxed tea into Boston Harbor. This is known as the Boston Tea Party.

The British sent soldiers into Boston and passed laws that closed down the harbor and Massachusetts's **legislature**. The angry people of Massachusetts then set up their own government, called the Provincial Congress. They gathered supplies to make sure their **militias** would be ready to fight against the British. They decided to store many of the supplies in Concord.

The colonists who took part in the Boston Tea Party, shown here, were part of a group called the Sons of Liberty. They protested British taxes and laws in the colonies.

WARNINGS FROM BOSTON

On the night of April 18, 1775, the British general Thomas Gage secretly sent soldiers from Boston to take the supplies from Concord. However, colonists in Boston learned the soldiers were headed to the countryside.

Bostonians William Dawes and Paul Revere left Boston to warn people that the British were coming.

Many people are taught that Revere was the only one who warned the colonists. This may be because Revere reached Lexington first or because a poem, "The Midnight Ride of Paul Revere," was written about him in the 1800s. However, William Dawes warned many colonists that night as well.

Although the British stopped Revere and Dawes after they left Lexington, a doctor named Samuel Prescott took the news to Concord that the British were coming.

10

Paul Revere rode through several Massachusetts towns between Boston and Lexington, warning the townspeople that the British were coming. His trip lasted around 2 hours.

THE MINUTEMEN

In Lexington, the colonists sent for the leader of the village's minutemen. Minutemen were special members of the militia who could come quickly when needed. The minutemen gathered on Lexington's common and waited for the British to arrive.

At daybreak, the British soldiers marched onto Lexington Common. There were about 10 times more British soldiers than minutemen, so the minutemen **retreated**. Though both the minutemen and the British were told by their leaders not to fire, a shot rang out. A few more shots followed. Then, the British opened fire on the retreating minutemen. Eight minutemen were killed.

Minutemen, such as the ones shown here, promised to be ready to fight the British within 2 minutes of receiving notice that they were needed.

WHO SHOT FIRST?

Some say the first shot was from a retreating minuteman. Others think a scared British soldier fired first. Some people think someone fired a warning shot into the air. Others suggest one of the retreating minutemen's guns went off by mistake.

Some people believe that an 18-year-old minuteman, named Solomon Brown, fired the first shot at Lexington from behind a wall after he had left the common.

The British soldiers said that an American fired the first shot. This helped explain why they had killed the retreating minutemen. Many minutemen claimed it was a British soldier who fired the first shot. This fed into their claim that they were just **defending** themselves. Though we know how the fighting at Lexington ended, nobody knows who started it.

Some people question if the fighting on Lexington Common would have happened had the first shot not been fired that morning.

ON TO CONCORD

After the fighting at Lexington ended, the British marched toward Concord. The minutemen of Concord and other nearby communities retreated in front of the British. Lieutenant Colonel Francis Smith, who led the British forces, told his men to keep the minutemen on the far side of the North Bridge, just outside Concord.

By this time, most of the supplies in Concord had already been moved. However, the British found and set fire to some bowls, tools, and gun parts. The minutemen, thinking the town was on fire, fought their way across the bridge. They killed three British soldiers and drove the rest back into Concord.

The British (left) were overpowered at the North Bridge. There were more minutemen (right) than British soldiers, and the British had formed a line that made them easy to hit.

THE LONG MARCH BACK

In the afternoon, Smith ordered the British to return to Boston. By this time, minutemen from all over eastern Massachusetts had come to fight. As the British made their long return trip, minutemen hid behind trees, rocks, and houses along the road and fired on the British.

The British soldiers were trained to march in rows and fight enemies the soldiers could see. They thought the Americans were fighting unfairly. The British fought poorly against the hidden minutemen, and dozens of British soldiers were killed. The remaining soldiers reached Boston only after more British soldiers arrived with **cannons** and drove away the minutemen.

The minutemen used their knowledge of the land to overcome the British. Here the minutemen are shown taking the British soldiers by surprise by firing from behind rocks and trees.

FREEDOM

Tales are often told about how a handful of minutemen defended themselves against the mighty British army. However, while the minutemen had been **outnumbered** in Lexington, there were more than 3,000 minutemen and fewer than 1,000 British soldiers on the march back to Boston! Also, many of the British soldiers had never fought before, while many minutemen had fought in the French and Indian War.

The minutemen knew the countryside well, unlike the British. They also learned to hide behind things while fighting when they fought in the French and Indian War.

Stories of the battle caused anger toward Great Britain. The American Revolution had begun! After Lexington and Concord, the fighting continued. Then, in July 1776, America became a free country.

The signing of the Declaration of Independence, shown here, marked the creation of the United States of America.

WHAT REALLY HAPPENED?

The battle of Lexington and Concord set off a war between England and the American colonies. It forced the colonists to rethink their ties to Great Britain. Without this battle, the United States might not be the country it is today.

The story of Lexington and Concord shows us how time can drown out the facts. It also shows us that certain facts are unknown. Who fired the first shot at Lexington? We may never know the truth. However, above all, the story shows us how the actions of a small group of people can change history.

GLOSSARY

cannons (KA-nunz) Large, heavy guns.

common (KAH-mun) Open land in a town or city not owned by any one person.

confused (kun-FYOOZD) Mixed up.

defending (dih-FEND-ing) Guarding from hurt.

legislature (LEH-jis-lay-chur) A body of people that has the power to make or pass laws.

militias (muh-LIH-shuz) Groups of people who are trained and ready to fight when needed.

outnumbered (owt-NUM-berd) Was greater in number than.

Parliament (PAR-leh-ment) The group in England that makes the country's laws.

protested (pruh-TEST-ed) Took part in acts of disagreement.

retreated (rih-TREET-ed) Backed away from a fight or another hard position.

soldiers (SOHL-jurz) People who are in an army.

INDEX

A
American Revolution, 4, 20

B
Boston, 4, 8, 10, 18, 20
British, 4, 8, 10, 12, 16, 18

C
colonies, 6, 8, 20, 22
colonists, 4, 6, 8, 10, 12, 22

common, 4, 12
country, 6, 20, 22

G
Great Britain, 6, 8, 20, 22

M
Massachusetts, 6, 8, 18
militia(s), 8, 12
minutemen, 12, 14, 16, 18, 20

P
Parliament, 6
Province of Massachusetts, 6

S
shot(s), 4, 12, 14, 22
soldier(s), 4, 8, 10, 12, 14, 16, 18, 20

W
war, 6, 22

WEB SITES

Due to the changing nature of Internet links, PowerKids Press has developed an online list of Web sites related to the subject of this book. This site is updated regularly. Please use this link to access the list:
www.powerkidslinks.com/wrh/lexcon/